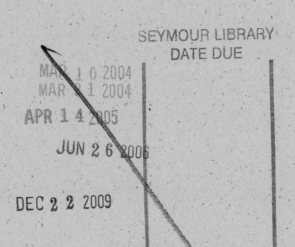

Levers may be used to extract oil deep in the ground

*L*evers

John Hudson Tiner

A⁺
Smart Apple Media

COPYRIGHT

❏ Published by Smart Apple Media

1980 Lookout Drive, North Mankato, MN 56003

Designed by Rita Marshall

Copyright © 2003 Smart Apple Media. International copyright reserved in all countries. No part of this book may be reproduced in any form without written permission from the publisher.

Printed in the United States of America

❏ Photographs by Richard Cummins, Horticultural Photography (Arthur N. Orans), Tom Myers, James P. Rowan, D. Jeanene Tiner

❏ Library of Congress Cataloging-in-Publication Data

Tiner, John Hudson. Levers / by John Tiner. p. cm. – (Simple machines)

Includes bibliographical references.

Summary: Describes how levers work and gives examples of levers in action.

❏ ISBN 1-58340-135-0

1. Levers–Juvenile literature. 2. Lifting and carrying–Juvenile literature.

[1. Levers.] I. Title.

TJ147 .T49 2002   621.8'11–dc21   2001049677

❏ First Edition 9 8 7 6 5 4 3 2 1

Levers

Making Jobs Easier   **6**

How Levers Work   **8**

Everyday Levers   **14**

Levers Working Together   **18**

Hands On: A Lever Experiment   **22**

Additional Information   **24**

Making Jobs Easier

Archimedes (ahr-kih-MEE-deez) was an ancient Greek scientist who did many experiments with **levers**. "Give me a long enough lever and a place to stand," he once said, "and I can move the world." ☐ Long ago, people had to use muscles to do all of their **work**. Most of the time, they used their own muscles. Sometimes they used the muscles of animals such as oxen and horses too. But what did they do when muscle power was not enough? They had to magnify their strength. In many cases, they put levers to work. ☐ A

person with ordinary strength could use a pry bar to move a

boulder. A pry bar was a type of lever. The pry bar was slipped

under the edge of the stone, and then the person pushed down

This man is using a lever to lift a heavy metal beam

on the bar. With this lever, the person could move a stone many times his or her own weight.

How Levers Work

A lever has three parts. It has a place for the load, or the thing being moved. It has a place for the effort, or the push or pull. And it has a point around which it turns, called the fulcrum (FUL-krum). A seesaw is an example of a lever. The seesaw is held in the middle at the fulcrum. ☐ The closer a load is to the fulcrum, the easier it is to move. A small effort

Levers were once used to pump underground water

A wheelbarrow shifts a load's weight onto the wheel

can move a large load. Levers exchange effort for distance.

Raising a heavy load a short distance takes a certain amount of

work. The work can be difficult if a person lifts the load

directly. The work can be easier if the person **A baseball bat is a lever that magnifies the speed of the end of the bat to hit the ball far.**

uses a lever instead and pushes the load

through a greater distance. ☐ Putting the

effort near the fulcrum moves a load more

quickly. For example, a person who is fishing holds a fishing

rod near the handle. The fishing rod, a lever, magnifies the

Fishing rods are levers that move quickly to cast bait

13

motion of the person's hands. A flip of the rod makes the tip move farther than the handle, and the fishing lure or bait is cast far out over the water.

Everyday Levers

A simple machine is a device that makes work easier. A lever is one kind of simple machine. A **force** is a push or pull. Levers change the direction of a force or make the force larger or smaller. ☐ We use levers every day. The back of a hammer, the claw, is a lever used to pull out nails. A person hooks the nail head with the claw and pulls on the handle. The

nail comes out easily. The nail is the load. The pull on the

handle is the effort. The fulcrum is the point where the claw

rests against the wood. ☐ A door is also a lever. The hinge is

The claw of a hammer can be used as a lever

the fulcrum, and the **resistance** of the door is the load. If the doorknob were next to the hinge, opening the door would be more difficult. The door is easier to open because the doorknob is as far from the hinge as possible.

☐ People have found uses for levers both big and small for thousands of years. Today, we use levers every time we open a soft drink can.

When sailors row a boat, they use the oars as levers. Water is the resistance.

The little ring that pops the tab is a kind of lever.

A doorknob is one end of the lever that opens a door

Levers Working Together

Many tools have two levers that share the same fulcrum. Scissors have two blades working together. The blades are levers, and the pin that holds the blades is the fulcrum. To cut thick paper, a person opens the scissors wide and puts the paper near the fulcrum. With the paper close to the fulcrum, less effort is needed to squeeze the handles, and cutting the paper is easier. ☐ Tweezers are two levers. The small pincers are at one end, and the fulcrum is at

Human jaws are two levers that work together. With the jaws, the teeth can grip and chew food.

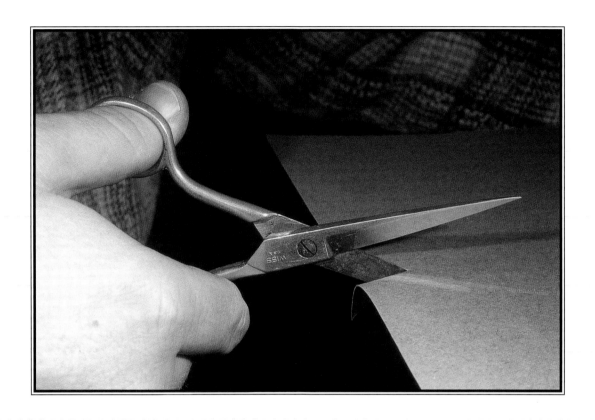

the other end. To use the tweezers, a person presses in at the

middle. The effort closes the tweezers to pluck or handle small

objects. Other levers are all around us. They include hand

Scissors are two sharp-edged levers that work together

brakes on bicycles, nutcrackers, pliers, and bars that open school doors. They also include hammers and other objects with handles that are swung to increase a person's hitting power. Even though these various levers may look different, they all do the same thing—make jobs easier by magnifying our strength.

The catapult was an ancient weapon used for throwing large objects. It was a lever combined with other simple machines.

A bicycle's hand brake is a commonly used lever

A Lever Experiment

This experiment will prove that a load is easier to lift when it is placed nearer a lever's fulcrum.

What You Need

A ruler   A pencil

A building block   About 50 pennies

What You Do

1. Place the pencil under the ruler at the six-inch (15 cm) mark.

2. Lay the wooden block on the end of the ruler that is marked 12 inches (30 cm).

3. Stack pennies at the other end. Stop when their weight raises the wooden block.

4. Count the number of pennies needed to raise the block.

5. Place the pencil under the ruler at the 10-inch (25 cm) mark. Repeat the experiment.

What You See

In the second experiment (step 5), fewer pennies are needed to raise the block. The ruler acts as a lever. The pencil is the fulcrum, the pennies are the effort, and the block is the load. It is easier to lift the load when it is nearer the fulcrum.

An oar is a lever that pushes a boat through water

Index

direction 14

distance 12, 16, 22

effort 8, 12, 15, 18, 22

fulcrum 8, 12, 15, 16, 18, 22

loads 8, 12, 15, 16, 22

pry bars 7-8

speed 13-14

strength 6, 7, 20

two levers 18-19

Words to Know

force (FORSS)—a push or pull that can move an object and do work

levers (LEH-verz)—simple machines with a pivot point and a place for the load and effort

resistance (rih-ZISS-tuhnss)—a force that acts against an effort

simple machine (SIM-puhl mah-SHEEN)—a basic device that changes the direction or amount of a force

work (WERK)—to apply a force to move an object

Read More

Ardley, Neil. *The Science Book of Machines*. London: Dorling Kindersley Limited, 1992.

Hodge, Deborah. *Simple Machines*. Buffalo, N.Y.: Kids Can Press, 1998.

Seller, Mick. *Wheels, Pulleys and Levers*. New York: Shooting Star Press, 1995.

Taylor, Barbara. *Force and Movement*. New York: Franklin Watts, 1990.

Internet Sites

Brain Pop™ Health and Science
http://www.brainpop.com/tech/
simplemachines/lever/index.weml

MIKIDS.COM: Levers
http://www.mikids.com/SMachines
Levers.htm

Museum of Science: The Elements of Machines
http://www.mos.org/sln/Leonardo/
InventorsToolbox.html